PowerKiDS
Readers
SEA FRIENDS

MANATEES

SAM DRUMLIN

PowerKiDS
press™

New York

Published in 2013 by The Rosen Publishing Group, Inc.
29 East 21st Street, New York, NY 10010

First Edition

Editor: Amelie von Zumbusch
Book Design: Liz Gloor and Colleen Bialecki

Photo Credits: Cover Perrine Doug/Perspectives/Getty Images; p. 5 Comstock/Thinkstock; p. 7 Steffen Foerster Photography/Shutterstock.com; p. 9 iStockphoto/Thinkstock; p. 11 Photo Researchers/Getty Images; pp. 13, 23 A Cotton Photo/Shutterstock.com; p. 15 Shane Gross/Shutterstock.com; p. 17 Undersea Discoveries/Shutterstock.com; p. 19 Douglas Faulkner/Photo Researchers/Getty Images; p. 21 Romarti/Shutterstock.com.

Library of Congress Cataloging-in-Publication Data

Drumlin, Sam.
  Manatees / by Sam Drumlin. — 1st ed.
      p. cm. — (Powerkids readers: sea friends)
  Includes index.
  ISBN 978-1-4488-9644-8 (library binding) — ISBN 978-1-4488-9746-9 (pbk.) — ISBN 978-1-4488-9747-6 (6-pack)
  1. Manatees—Juvenile literature. I. Title.
  QL737.S63D78 2013
  599.55—dc23
                                            2012022770

Manufactured in the United States of America

CPSIA Compliance Information: Batch #W13PK3: For Further Information contact Rosen Publishing, New York, New York at 1-800-237-9932

CONTENTS

Manatees live in warm water.

They can live in rivers or in the sea.

They are also called sea cows.

There are three kinds
of manatees.

They eat **plants**.

They are big and gentle.

Boats often hurt them.

Babies are **calves**.

They drink milk.

21

They can live for up to 60 years.

WORDS TO KNOW

calf

manatee

plants

INDEX

WEBSITES

Due to the changing nature of Internet links, PowerKids Press has developed an online list of websites related to the subject of this book. This site is updated regularly. Please use this link to access the list:
www.powerkidslinks.com/pkrsf/mana/